Contents

Say the Sounds	4
Tricky Words	5
Meet the Characters	6
The Bird House	7
Daisy and Buttercup	25
The New Kitten	43
An Inter-Hive Match	61
The Maize Maze	79
Beach Rescue	97
Book Review	116
Character Review	118

This book belongs to

Tricky Words

- many
- any
- before
- more
- other
- were
- because
- want
- made
- saw
- would
- their
- put
- should
- could
- right
- two
- goes
- four
- does

The Bird House

Snake, Inky and Bee had gone for a walk in the Vowel Forest. It had been raining all day the day before, and there had been a big storm in the night. Twigs and leaves littered the forest floor.

It was still very damp underfoot. Bee ran about and kicked at the piles of leaves.
"I am glad I was safe inside," hissed Snake, looking around.

"Yes," agreed Inky. "I had to turn Phonic off. There was a lot of lightning."

"Did he not want to come out with us today?" said Snake.

"No," Inky shook her head. "He said it was still too wet, but he will want to know all about what happened while he was switched off."

A bit further along, a tree had been blown down. There were leaves and twigs all around, and the trunk of the tree was lying on the ground.

"Wow!" said Snake, looking at the jagged tree stump. "What a mess!"

Wow!

Snake started to slither along the fallen tree trunk. As he got to the middle, a small bird burst out from the leaves in the treetop. She started to dive bomb Snake, tweeting and shouting, "Go away, you horrid Snake!"

"Ow! What? Help!" cried Snake in surprise, ducking to avoid the little bird's attack. As the bird continued to dive bomb him, Snake slipped off the trunk and landed in a heap.

Inky rushed to him to see if he was all right. Snake sat up, looking dazed, and said, "What did I do?"

Inky shook her head. "Perhaps the bird has a nest with some eggs in that tree. I expect she thinks you might want to eat them. Bee is chatting to her. Perhaps she can see what the problem is."

"What's the matter?" said Inky when Bee came back to them.

"The little bird has a nest and two chicks in the tree," explained Bee. "While the tree was still standing, they were safe. She is very upset," she added.

"Yes, I gathered that," muttered Snake.

"Sh!" said Inky.

"She cannot leave her chicks to go and collect food because they are not safe on the ground," Bee continued. "Then she saw Snake slithering along and she wanted to stop him getting as far as her nest."

"I was not slithering up to her nest!" spluttered Snake, indignantly. "I was just looking around."

"I know that, and Inky knows that, but she does not," said Bee, pointing to the little bird.

"Well, go and tell her," prompted Snake.

Inky ran back to get Phonic to see if he could help.

"Well," said Phonic when it had all been explained. "We have two problems here. One, the chicks need to be fed and guarded from harm, and two, the bird needs to build a new nest in another tree."

So, for the next week, Inky and Bee helped the little bird by staying with the chicks, while she went out and collected food for them.

Snake and Phonic shut themselves away in the shed and started building a new home for the bird and her family.

"I haven't seen Snake and Phonic out in the forest collecting sticks and things for my new nest," chirped the little bird one morning.

What are they doing?

"Buzz," went Bee. "Before they began, they spent some time discussing how to make the ultimate birdhouse, and er... I do not think it will be quite the same as your old nest."

"Good morning," hissed Snake, slithering up. "If you are ready, you can settle into your new home today."

"Goody," twittered the bird, "but where is it? I haven't seen you or a new nest anywhere in this part of the forest."

"Well," said Snake, "we have put your new home in the big tree in the garden. It should be safe there, and we can still help with your chicks."

Inky, Bee, the bird and her chicks stood looking at the new home that Snake and Phonic had made.

"It's very different," said the bird.

"Try it," said Phonic. "We tried to make it better than your old nest. It has a lot more room and it will stay dry in all weathers."

They helped the bird get her chicks into the house.

"You have put lots of soft stuff inside," she said, "and you are right. A roof will mean we will not get wet. It's perfect! Thank you so much. I never dreamed I would ever live in a house like this one!"

Daisy and Buttercup

Farmer Green keeps a herd of cows on Moat Farm. He has to milk them every morning and every evening.

"Come on, come on!" he shouts, and the cows line up outside the milking shed.

Daisy and Buttercup are two of Farmer Green's cows. In the summer, they spend their time on the marshes. They come back to the farm when Farmer Green calls them.

One day, Daisy and Buttercup stood on the marsh, chewing the cud and chatting. They had spent some time looking for thistles but had not found any. Fresh thistles were what Buttercup liked best.

As they ambled along the side of a stream, Buttercup spotted a very big thistle. It was growing at the bottom of the bank, down by the stream.

"Ooh! Look at that thistle," she mooed to Daisy.

"Mmmm, what a shame it is so far down the bank. You will never reach it," said Daisy.

"I think I might... just," mooed Buttercup, stretching her neck down.

"You will never get it," Daisy snorted and shook her head.

"Yes I will," insisted Buttercup. "Just a little further. If I take one more step and stretch a little more, it's mine."

With that, Buttercup took one more step and tumbled down the bank and into the stream.

"Help!" she mooed as she struggled to get out. But the bottom of the stream was soft, and Buttercup's hooves just sank further and further into the soft mud.

"Stay still," shouted Daisy from the top of the bank, "I will get help," and she started mooing as loudly as she could.

Farmer Green soon arrived to see what all the noise was about.

"What's up?" he said to Daisy. "Where is Buttercup? You two are always together."

Daisy peered down the bank and mooed again. Farmer Green peered down the bank too.

"Buttercup!" he exclaimed. "What are you doing down there?"

Buttercup stood in the stream looking very sad, muddy and wet. Farmer Green slithered down the bank and tried to get Buttercup out. But it was no good. Buttercup was stuck!

"Can we help?"
Farmer Green looked up and saw a fireman peering down from the other side of the bank.

"Someone saw a cow stuck in a stream and called us," he continued.

"If you can," said Farmer Green. "I cannot get her out, and I cannot get my tractor down here as the ground is too soft. Your truck would get stuck too. I do not know how we can get her out."

The fireman came down the bank and looked at Buttercup.

"Hand that long ladder down, and as much rope as we have," he called up.

They put the ladder so it lay across the stream from bank to bank. One of the firemen crawled along the ladder. Another one put on long rubber boots and walked into the stream. Between them, they got a long thick rope around Buttercup's middle.

Wow!

All the firemen and Farmer Green heaved and heaved. Buttercup struggled to help, and with a squish and a squelch she was free. They heaved some more and hauled Buttercup back up the bank.

"Hooray!" everyone cried.

The firemen hosed down a very muddy and soggy-looking Buttercup. Farmer Green thanked them and helped them pack away all their things. Then he waved them goodbye as they drove off.

Turning back to Buttercup, he said, "Come on, old girl. You had better thank Daisy for getting help so quickly. It would have become very cold in there. Let's go back to the farm and you can have something to eat in safety!"

What's in the book?

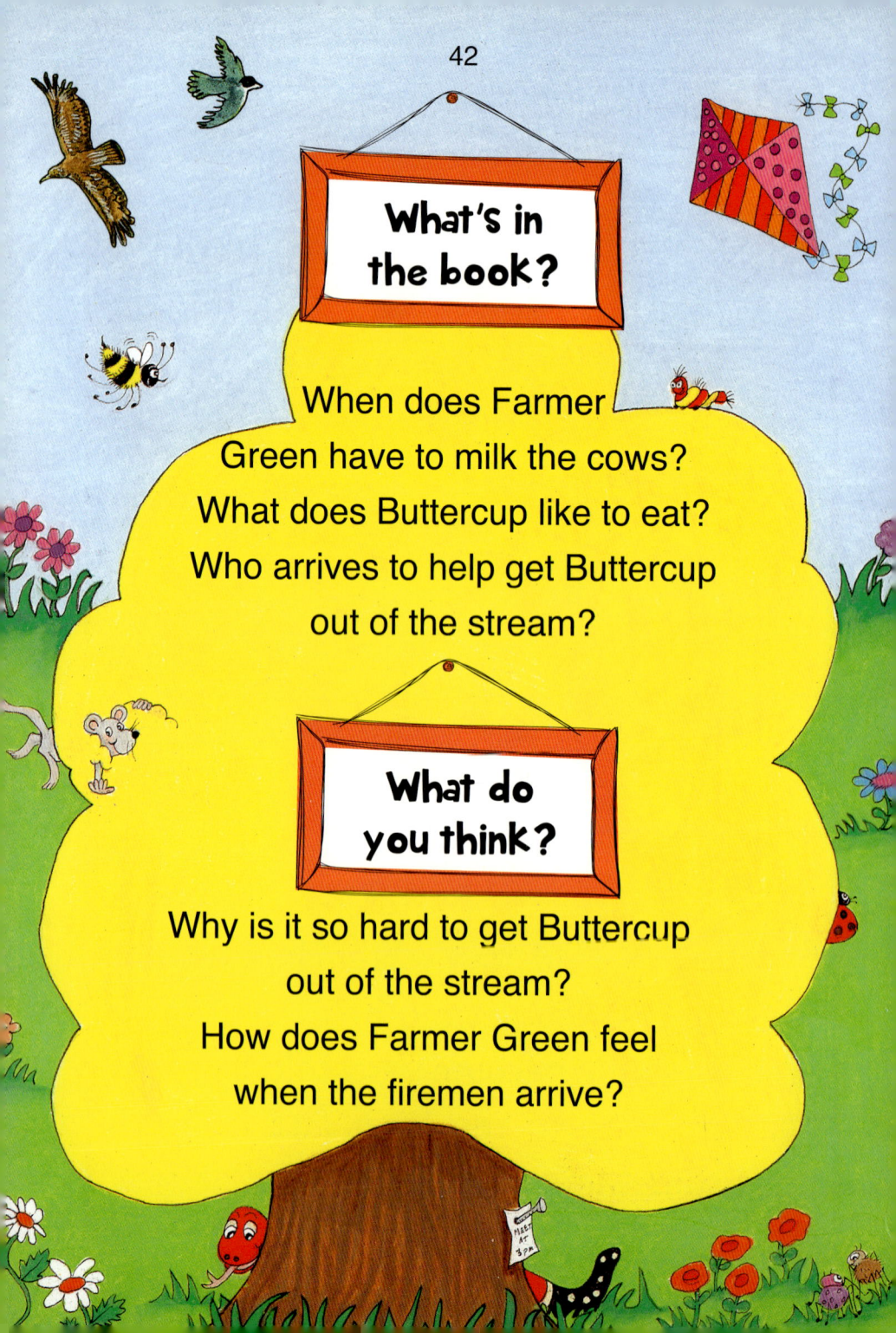

When does Farmer Green have to milk the cows?
What does Buttercup like to eat?
Who arrives to help get Buttercup out of the stream?

What do you think?

Why is it so hard to get Buttercup out of the stream?
How does Farmer Green feel when the firemen arrive?

The New Kitten

Zack, Jess and Rags were playing outside. Zack and Rags were throwing a ball and Jess was on the swing. Suddenly, Jess saw something in the flowers by the gate.

She got off the swing and went to look. Sitting by the gate was a little kitten. It looked very sad and thin.

"You poor thing!" cried Jess.

Zack and Rags came across to see what she was looking at.

As soon as Rags saw the kitten, he started barking. The kitten turned and ran, squeezing under the gate. Zack and Jess looked and looked, but they could not see where the kitten had gone.

Jess kept looking and calling for the kitten for the rest of the day, but she could not see it. That night, before she went to bed, she went out and looked for the kitten again.

Kitty!

The next evening, Jess and Zack's granny rang.

"Hello, Jess," she said. "I came around this morning, but everyone was out. Dad told me about the kitten when I spoke to him yesterday. How did you get it to come in?"

"What do you mean?" said Jess. "It ran off. We could not see it."

"Well," said Granny, "when I looked in your back door, there was a kitten sitting there, looking back at me!"

Jess and Zack looked everywhere they could think of in the house. They tried looking under the beds and all around the kitchen, but they could not see the kitten.

Sniff!

They stood very still and listened, but there was no sound. Rags sniffed around too, but still the kitten was nowhere to be seen.

The next evening, Granny and Gramps came for dinner. Dad said to Granny, "I think you were seeing things. There is no kitten in here."

Just wait and see!

"I tell you, I saw a kitten sitting in the kitchen. I did not make a mistake," said Granny, firmly. "Just you wait and see!"

The next Saturday, Zack and Jess took Rags for a long walk. They walked a long way and stopped to have lunch. As they were eating, Dad rang.

"You found it!"

"Guess what I have just found!" he said.
"The kitten!" cried Jess, happily.
"Yes," said Dad, "I shall have to say sorry to Granny. She was right!"

"I will put him outside so he can go home," said Dad.

"No, please," begged Jess. "Wait until we get home. I want to see him."

Where is he?

They hurried home as quickly as they could. Zack and Jess burst in the back door.

"Where have you put the kitten?" called Jess.

"In there," said Dad, pointing.

"There he is!"

Zack and Jess went in and looked at the kitten.

"He seems very frightened," said Dad.

"And very small and thin," added Zack.

"What if he does not have a home to go back to?" said Jess.

"Well, we are not keeping him," said Dad, firmly. "He can stay for now but you had better start looking for his home tomorrow."

Meeow

Jess stroked and cuddled the kitten all evening and Zack made a bed for him from an old box.

The next day, Zack, Jess and Dad went everywhere they could think of, but no one had lost a kitten.

They put a note up at the animal hospital and on the tree outside their house, but no one called them.

Look!

When Dad came in the following evening, there was a note taped to the door.

"*Please can we keep him?*" he read. As he hung his coat up, he saw another note. "*He is so very small. Please, please, please can we keep him?*"

In the sitting room was yet another note.
   "*He is very good. We will feed and brush him.*"

Keep him?

Zzzzz

   Dad groaned and looked at the small bundle of fur curled up in the box-bed Zack had made.

When Zack and Jess came down for breakfast the next morning, they found notes on their dishes.

"Yes, you can!" read Zack.

"What will you call him?" read Jess.

"Wow! Thank you, thank you!" she squealed. "His name is Blackberry," she cried, picking the kitten up and hugging him.

What's in the book?

Where does Jess first see the kitten?

Who looks through the back door and sees the kitten?

Where do the children put up notes about the lost kitten?

What do you think?

Why is the kitten scared of Rags at the beginning?

Where do you think the kitten was hiding in the house?

An Inter-Hive Match

Inky was in the garden, looking at the flowers and listening to the buzzing of the bees.

What are you doing?

The buzzing was getting louder and Inky could see Bee jogging around the side of the shed. Inky looked puzzled and called out to Bee, "What are you doing? Bees fly, not jog!"

"I am in training," called back Bee, and she jogged off.

Inky frowned. Then Snake arrived, looking puzzled.

"Have you ever seen a bee running?" he enquired.

"Funny you should say that," said Inky, "but yes, just now."

"Bees never run anywhere," said Snake.

"No," agreed Inky. "What can Bee be up to?"

"I think we should amble across to Bee's hive and see what is going on," said Snake.

As they got to the hive, they could see lots of bees, and they were all running, jumping and skipping.

"What are they all doing?" hissed Snake to Inky. "You would think they were fit already, with all that buzzing about they do!"

They found Bee sitting by the door of the hive, panting.

"What has got into all you bees?" said Snake. "I know you bees are always doing things, but this is silly."

"I feel out of breath just looking at you all," added Inky.

"Puff!"

"We are in training," gasped Bee.

"In training!" exclaimed Inky and Snake. "For what?"

"The inter-hive soccer match. Our hive plays the hive on the other side of the orchard. It's for the Pollen Cup."

"Only the best players get picked for the team," continued Bee, "and every bee wants to play. The orchard hive have been the winners three times. We are determined to beat them. The team will be picked tomorrow."

Snake and Inky wished Bee good luck.

"I made it! I made it!" buzzed Bee as she rushed up to Inky and Snake the next day.

"Made what?" said Snake from where he was lying, enjoying the sun. "Can we eat it? I could do with a snack."

"No, silly," buzzed Bee. "I made the soccer team. I am going to play in the match!"

On Saturday, Inky and Snake made their way to the orchard, where the match was to be played. The bees were all waiting for the match to start.

Clap!

Cheer!

Cheer!

Clap!

Suddenly, there was a loud buzzing cheer from the crowd and the two teams ran out onto the pitch. Bee's team had a red strip, and the orchard hive's team were in blue.

The referee blew his whistle and the match began. Bee's red team scored first, and it was Bee who scored the goal!
    Snake, Inky and all the red supporters cheered loudly, but then the blue team got the ball.

Yes!

Bee tackled, got the ball and ran down the wing. Just before she reached the goal, she was tackled and the blue team got the ball again.

Whoops!

Got it!

The ball crossed the Reds' goal and a bee from the Blues kicked it. The Reds' supporters groaned, but the keeper saved the ball. Inky and Snake clapped and cheered with the rest of the Reds.

The red team kicked off quickly and hurtled down the pitch. A bee from the blue team rushed and tackled.

The Blues were now heading back down to the goal, while the orchard hive supporters clapped and shouted. Then a big bee from the blue team kicked and scored!

When the whistle blew at the end of the match, the score was two-two. It was a draw.

"What happens now?" said Inky.

"It goes to a penalty shoot-out," hissed Snake.

"A what?" said Inky.

"The teams take it in turns to shoot at the goal and the first team to miss has lost the game," hissed back Snake.

The orchard hive went first and scored. Then it was Bee's turn. She kicked and scored. Snake and Inky clapped.

The next two bees also scored and then the orchard hive scored again. A bee from the Reds stepped up, kicked the ball and missed!

Snake, Inky and all the Reds groaned. Bee's hive had lost.

Snake and Inky went to see Bee. To their surprise, she was surrounded by the other bees and they were all grinning.

"We came to see how you were," said Inky. "You look quite happy, considering your team lost."

"Good for you!"

"Well," buzzed Bee, "it would have been good to win, but I did get picked for the team, and we played really well, and it was the best match ever! I had a really good time and I cannot wait for the next match!"

What's in the book?

What are the bees training for?
Which bees are wearing blue?
Which team wins the match?

What do you think?

Why does Bee get picked for the team?
Is it important to win?

The Maize Maze

Zack and Jess are visiting Farmer Green's Maize Maze. They stand in line and wait. Sally, Farmer Green's wife, gives them their tickets.

"As you go round the maze, there are some clues," says Sally. "You have to guess what shape the maze is."

"Each clue has a number and comes with a rubber stamp. Stamp the box on your card next to that number. That way you can check you have found all the clues. Good luck!" says Sally, with a smile.

Zack and Jess thank her and run into the maze.

"This way," calls Zack, running off to the right. He turns right again and then waits for Jess at the next turning. "Which way shall we go?" he says, as she stops.

This way!

Jess looks around.

"I never knew maize grew this tall," she says. "You really cannot see where you are," she continues, jumping up and down.

"Where are we?"

"Look! Corn!"

"Look!" says Zack, pointing. "I can see corn on the cob. Perhaps we can have some for dinner when we finish the maze."

"Let's turn right again and see where it goes," says Jess. It leads them to their first clue. There is a small plastic box, marked with the number two. Zack takes the lid off and Jess takes out the clue.

"Read it!"

"Go on! Read it aloud," he says.

"*I live here*," reads Jess. "That's easy, then. It has to be Farmer Green!"

"Mmmm, wait a bit," says Zack. "Farmer Green is not the only living thing on the farm. What about all the animals? Come on, let's stamp our card and look for another clue."

They run along the maze and stop at the next crossroads.

Right?

Left?

"I think we should turn left this time, not right," says Jess.
"OK," agrees Zack, and off they go.

Further along, they meet two boys hurrying back.

"We found a clue down there," call the boys, pointing back the way they have just come.

"Thanks," call Zack and Jess as they hurry on.

This time, Zack and Jess see a box with the number four on it.

"*I have this number of legs,*" reads out Zack.

"Mmmm, four legs. Definitely not Farmer Green then," giggles Jess.

Hee! Hee!

They continue around the maze. They turn left and then right again.

"I think we must be at the other side of the maze now," says Jess.

"Yes," agrees Zack, "and look! I can see another clue."

Another clue!

Cluck!

"Right," says Zack. "So it lives on the farm, it has four legs, and this one says, *'I get very cross.'*"

Jess takes the rubber stamp out of the box and stamps their card.

They carry on, collecting more clues. Zack looks up at a bird soaring across the sky.

"Wouldn't it be fantastic if we could fly like that bird and look down on the maze?"

"Yes," agrees Jess. "Then we could see what shape it is without having to solve all the clues."

"Well, by the look of it we only have one more clue to solve, as we have put a stamp in all the rest of the boxes," says Zack.

Jess looks. "All the stamps are of animals that live on the farm - a chicken, a horse, a sheep, a dog and a cow."

"One more clue to go, and there it is!" Zack points down a track to the side. They turn and dash down the track. Zack reaches the box first.

"What does it say, what does it say?" says Jess, trying to see the clue.

Quick!

Buzzz!

Here they come!

"OK, OK, wait and listen to the clue because I think I have solved the puzzle," smiles Zack. *"I am not a kid,"* he reads.

I can guess!

Jess smiles too. "I can guess what shape the maze is. Come on, let's go and look for the way out."

"You did it!"

They hand their card to Sally.

"Good," says Sally, "you have all the stamps here, so you get a lollipop each. But, have you solved the clues?"

"Yes!" they say, nodding and grinning. "The maze is in the shape of the bad-tempered goat!"

What's in the book?

What do the children have to guess?
What is growing on the maize?
How many clues do the children have to find?

What do you think?

Why would it be easy for a bird to solve all the clues?
Why does the last clue say 'I am not a kid'?

Beach Rescue

Bee, Inky and Snake were going to the beach. Phonic had refused to go as the sand would get everywhere and there would be far too much wet stuff around.

"Today, I am happy to stay at home and play with one of my games," he said. He hoped the others would have a good time.

Inky, Bee and Snake arrived at the beach and looked around for a good spot to sit down.

"There!" said Bee, pointing. "We can lean against those rocks."

"Yes," agreed Inky, nodding, "and we are not too far away from the sea." They put their things down and quickly set up camp.

"Come on, I want to go and look among the rocks," said Snake, slithering off. Bee picked up a bucket and a fishing net and followed Snake onto the rocks.

"Look at this," called Snake. "This pool is enormous and there are lots of things living in it."

Here I come!

Bee and Inky scrambled quickly across the rocks to join Snake.

"Look at those little fish," said Bee. "Good job I have the net!"

"Mmmmm," hissed Snake, licking his lips.

Where?

"Look at that big shrimp!" exclaimed Inky.

"Where?" said Bee.

"Under that big rock. You can just see its head and feelers sticking out."

"Mmmmmmm," hissed Snake again with a big smile.

They pottered around the rocks and pools for some time. Then they went back to the beach where they had left their things, sat down and had a drink.

Hic!

Yum, yum.

"I am hot," said Inky, jumping up. "I feel like surfing! Who wants to come with me?"

"Not me," said Bee. "I am not a good swimmer and I do not like getting my wings wet."

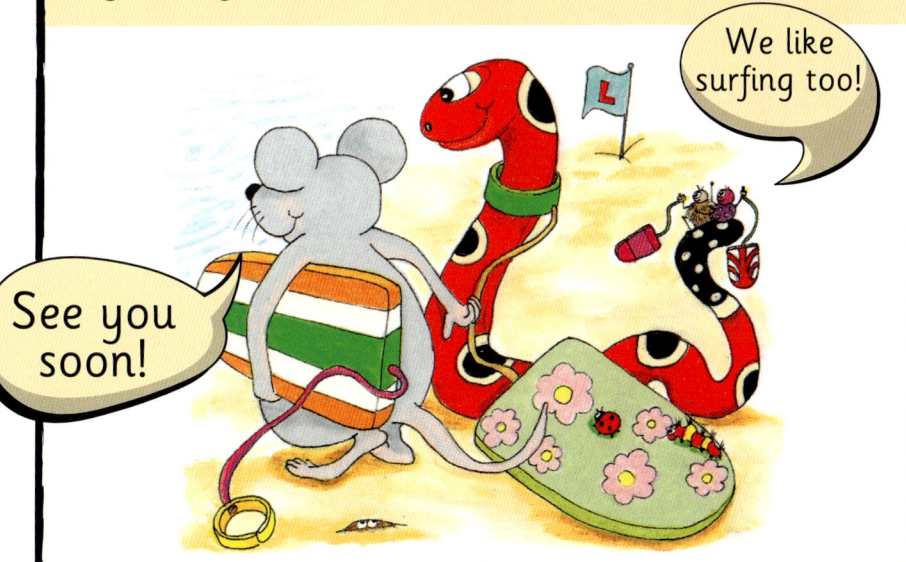

We like surfing too!

See you soon!

Inky and Snake set off, heading for the spot between the flags where the lifeguards were. They turned and waved at Bee before splashing into the sea.

They paddled around in the sea for a while, looking at the other swimmers and surfers.

"The lifeguards look really small from out here," said Snake.

"Bee looks smaller still," said Inky and waved at her.

Bee waved back and lay down to enjoy the sun as Snake and Inky began to surf.

Bee!

Here we are!

"Let's surf one more time and then we had better go back," said Inky as Snake swam back to her. They looked back at the beach.

"Gosh!" said Snake. "Look how far the tide has come in. It is right at the top of the beach."

"Yes," said Inky, "and I cannot see Bee at all," she continued.

Where is Bee?

Just then, two of the lifeguards on the beach started shouting and pointing out to sea. Snake and Inky looked to where they were pointing. There, far out to sea, was a rubber ring with someone in it. That someone waved frantically.

Inky squinted at the ring. "No!" she cried. "That's Bee out there! Whatever is she doing so far out to sea?"

Come back!

Inky started swimming out to Bee. Snake grabbed her by the tail and hauled her back.

"Stop being silly," he hissed. "The lifeguards have seen her and they will rescue her. If you swim out there, they may have to rescue you too."

Snake and Inky stood on the beach with the other swimmers and surfers. They were all looking at Bee, who was floating further and further out to sea.

"Bee! Bee!" cried Inky, wringing her paws. "I cannot understand why she went in the sea at all. She does so hate getting her wings wet."

Just then, there was another noise: a wump, wump, wump, wump sound. A seagull ran along the beach, jumped, and started flying. It flew out to sea, then stopped just where Bee was floating.

The seagull dived down and landed next to Bee. He picked her up with his beak, flapped his wings and headed back to shore.

"Hooray!" A big cheer went up as they landed on the beach. The gull put Bee down on the sand. She sat there looking very bedraggled. Inky and Snake ran and hugged her.

Sniff!

"I am so glad you are safe," said Inky, "but whatever were you doing so far out to sea?"

"I did not mean to go out to sea," sobbed Bee. "The tide came in and I had to put all our things further up the beach. I was only going to tell you where I was, but I could not see you or Snake. Soon I was being swept out to sea, and by then my wings were wet and I could not fly back."

There, there.

"Why has it gone dark?"

"That's better."

Bee, Inky and Snake thanked the seagull and the lifeguards. Then Inky and Snake helped the wet and bedraggled Bee back up the beach to their things.

They quickly packed up and went home, where Bee could dry off, and they could tell the story of the dramatic seaside rescue.

What's in the book?

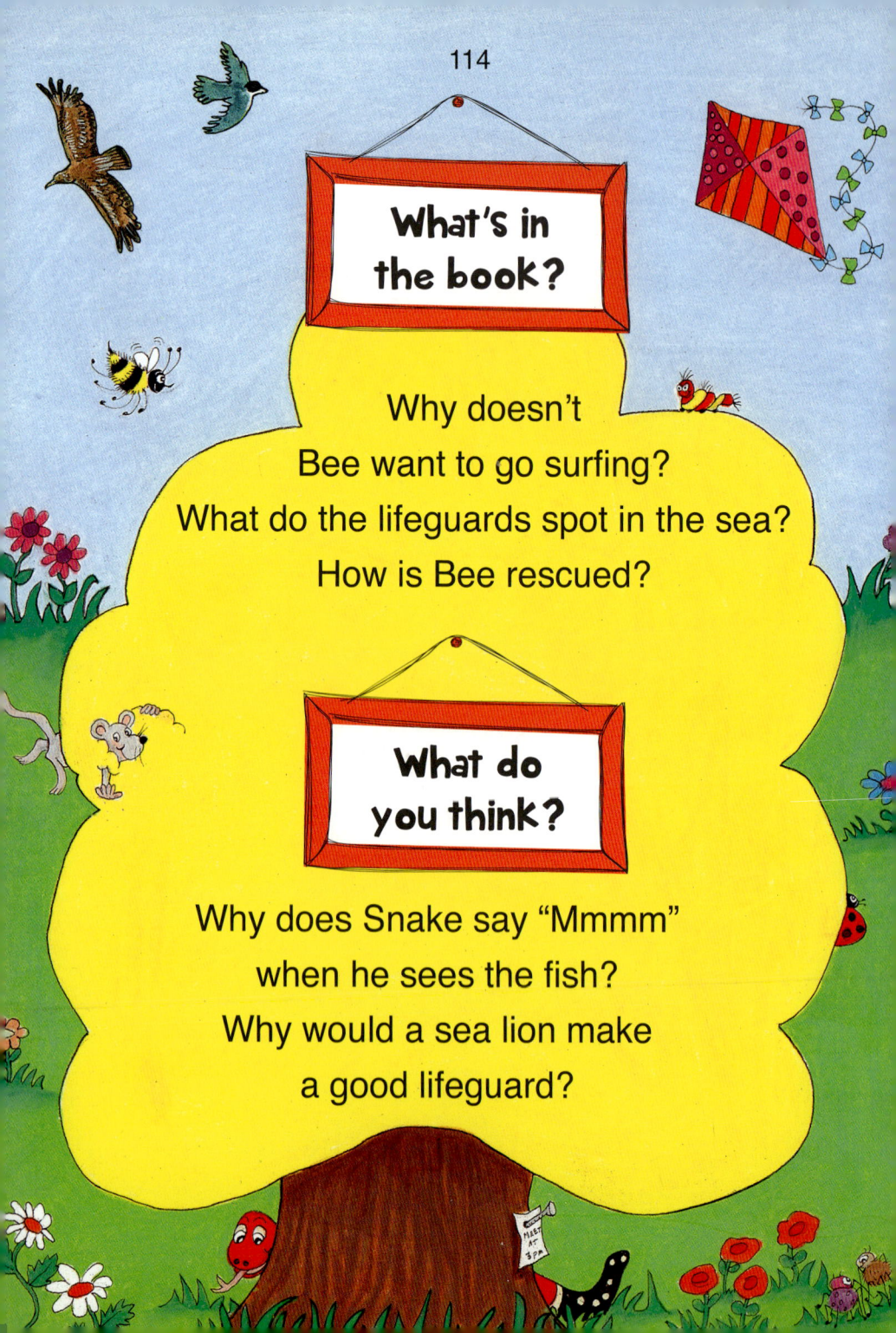

Why doesn't
Bee want to go surfing?
What do the lifeguards spot in the sea?
How is Bee rescued?

What do you think?

Why does Snake say "Mmmm"
when he sees the fish?
Why would a sea lion make
a good lifeguard?

Parents

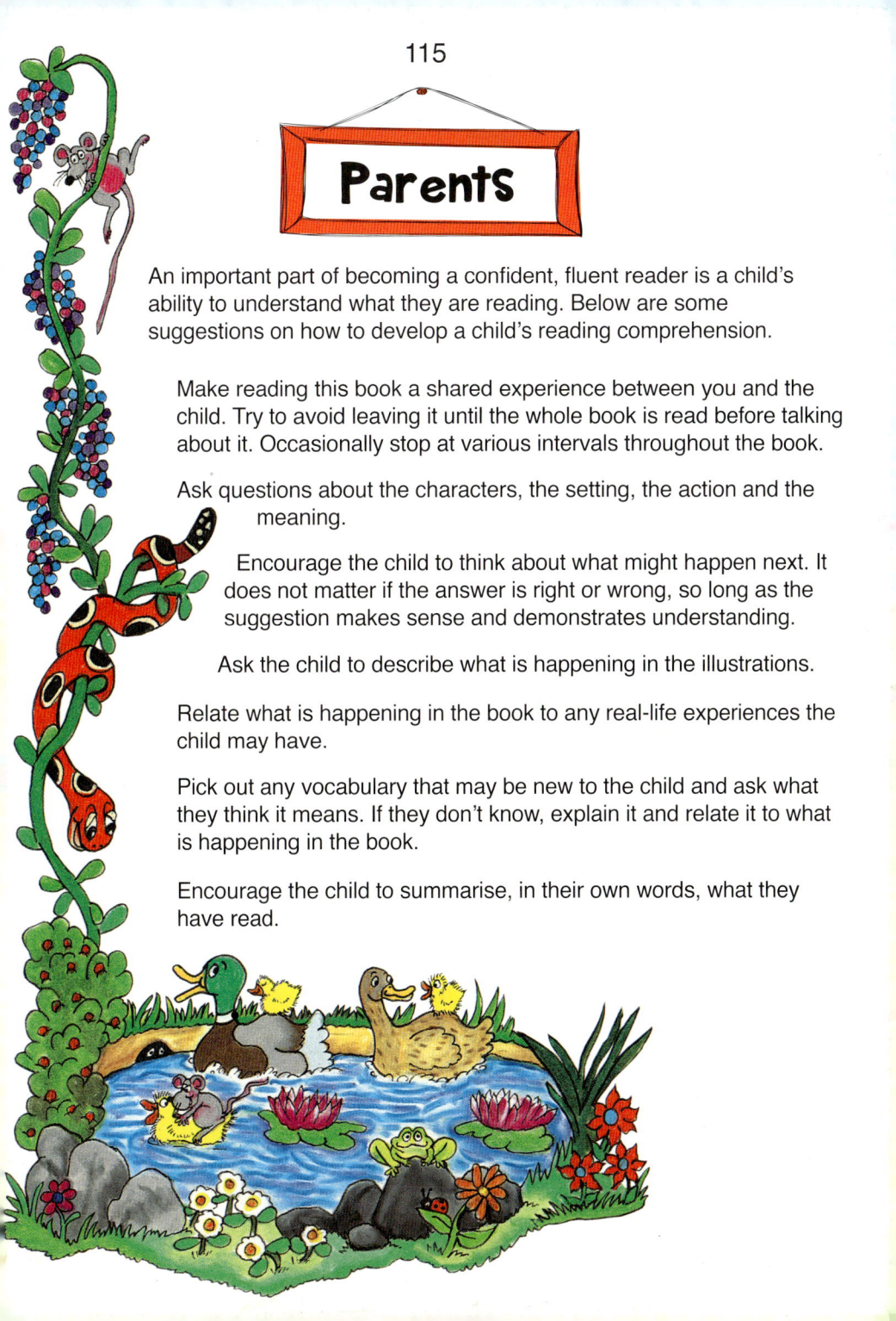

An important part of becoming a confident, fluent reader is a child's ability to understand what they are reading. Below are some suggestions on how to develop a child's reading comprehension.

Make reading this book a shared experience between you and the child. Try to avoid leaving it until the whole book is read before talking about it. Occasionally stop at various intervals throughout the book.

Ask questions about the characters, the setting, the action and the meaning.

Encourage the child to think about what might happen next. It does not matter if the answer is right or wrong, so long as the suggestion makes sense and demonstrates understanding.

Ask the child to describe what is happening in the illustrations.

Relate what is happening in the book to any real-life experiences the child may have.

Pick out any vocabulary that may be new to the child and ask what they think it means. If they don't know, explain it and relate it to what is happening in the book.

Encourage the child to summarise, in their own words, what they have read.

Book Review

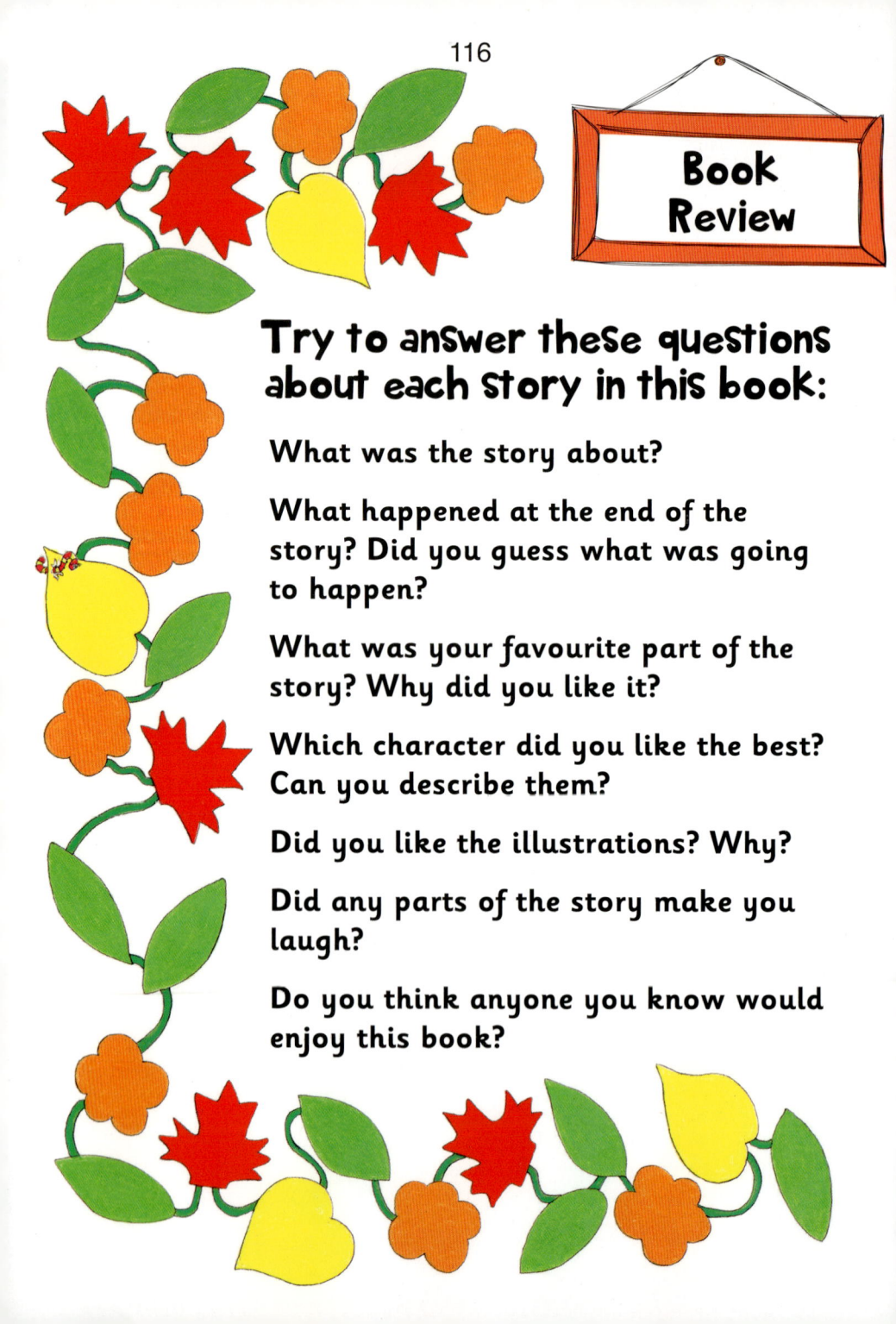

Try to answer these questions about each story in this book:

What was the story about?

What happened at the end of the story? Did you guess what was going to happen?

What was your favourite part of the story? Why did you like it?

Which character did you like the best? Can you describe them?

Did you like the illustrations? Why?

Did any parts of the story make you laugh?

Do you think anyone you know would enjoy this book?

Could you re-tell the story in your own words?

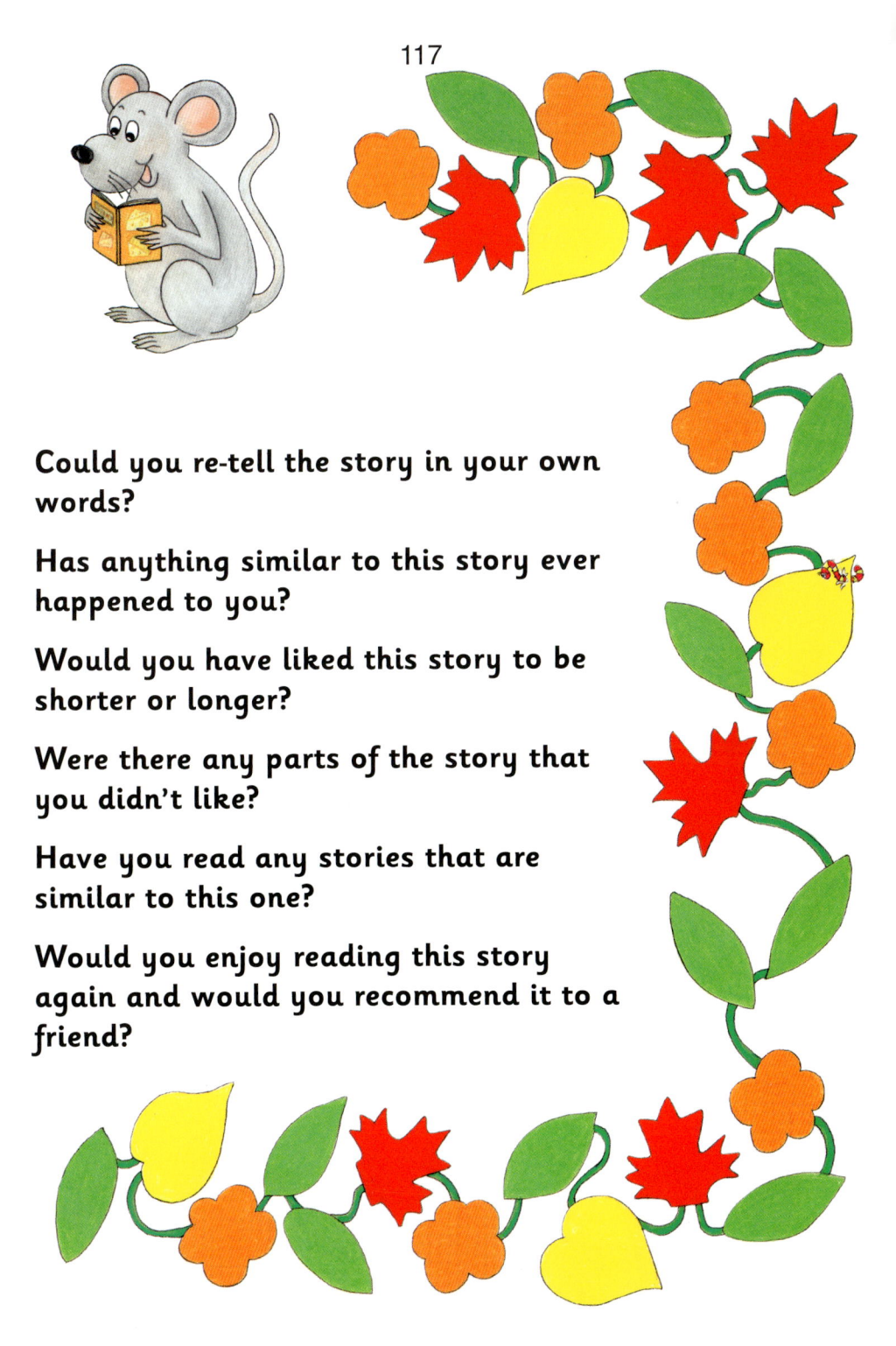

Has anything similar to this story ever happened to you?

Would you have liked this story to be shorter or longer?

Were there any parts of the story that you didn't like?

Have you read any stories that are similar to this one?

Would you enjoy reading this story again and would you recommend it to a friend?

Character Review

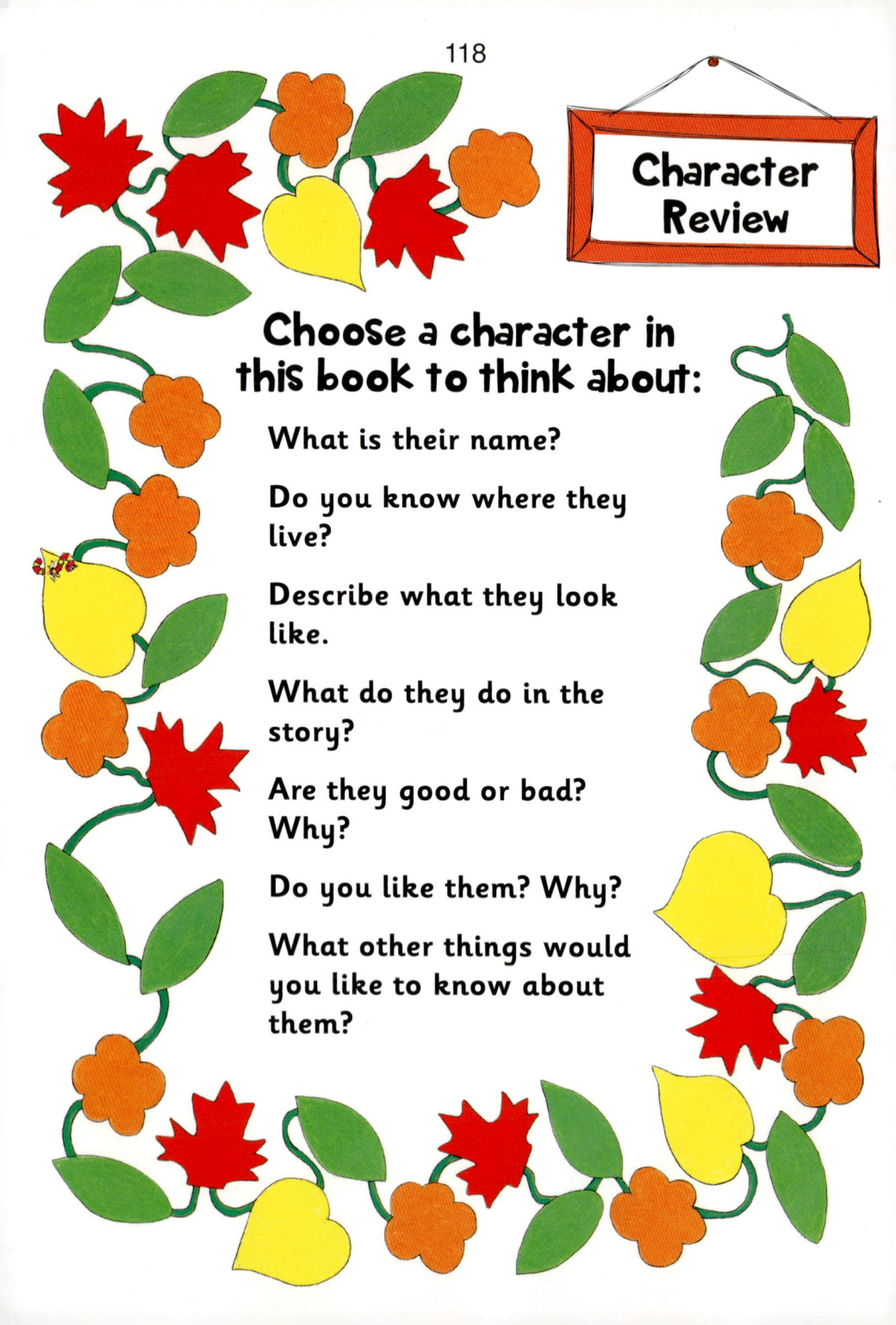

Choose a character in this book to think about:

What is their name?

Do you know where they live?

Describe what they look like.

What do they do in the story?

Are they good or bad? Why?

Do you like them? Why?

What other things would you like to know about them?